THE LIFE & TIMES OF

Horatio Nelson

BY
James Brown

This edition first published by
Parragon Book Service Ltd in 1996

Parragon Book Service Ltd
Unit 13–17 Avonbridge Trading Estate
Atlantic Road, Avonmouth
Bristol BS11 9QD

Produced by Magpie Books,
an imprint of Robinson Publishing

Copyright © Parragon Book Service Ltd 1996

Illustrations courtesy of: Bridgeman Art Library; Hulton
Deutsch Collection; Peter Newark's Historical Pictures

All rights reserved. This book is sold subject to the
condition that it shall not, by way of trade or otherwise,
be lent, resold, hired out or otherwise circulated
without the publisher's prior consent in any form of
binding or cover other than that in which it is published
and without similar condition being imposed on
the subsequent purchaser.

ISBN 0 75251 556 X

A copy of the British Library Cataloguing in Publication
Data is available from the British Library.

Typeset by Whitelaw & Palmer Ltd, Glasgow
Printed in Singapore

'POOR HORATIO'

Into the comparatively settled and increasingly secular world of the mid-eighteenth century was born, on 29 September 1758, a man whose career would challenge the conventional wisdom. Laurence Olivier once remarked, thinking of his own childhood, that a background of genteel poverty is a tremendous spur to ambition. Like Olivier, who would later bring his instinct for heroism to his glamorous portrayal of Nelson (in the film *Lady Hamilton*),

Horatio Nelson was the son of an impoverished clergyman. The Reverend Edmund Nelson was the rector of Burnham Thorpe in Norfolk. The Nelsons had a background in the Church, while through his wife, Catherine, Edmund Nelson had connections with one of the most powerful families in England, the Walpoles. Even so, with nothing but Edmund's stipend, and with eight sons to provide for (three other children had died in infancy), the Nelsons' life was austere. It was an austerity that the death of Mrs Nelson in 1767 can have done nothing to alleviate.

However, Nelson's childhood was not a long one. One of his uncles was in the Royal Navy; indeed, Captain Maurice Suckling was reckoned a hero, at least in his sister's family. Every year on 21 October they marked the

Nelson by Sir William Beechey

anniversary of his combat with a superior French fleet off the West Indies in 1759. It is hard not to imagine the idea of adding to the family's list of glorious feats being planted in Nelson's mind by this family ritual. But the existence of a near relation with some influence in this profession had much more practical importance in Nelson's world. As a widower, Edmund Nelson could not afford to neglect such contacts in the struggle to provide for his large family. However, it was, according to one story, Nelson's own idea that he was the son who should be sent to sea, though the idea rather surprised his Uncle Maurice, who judged his nephew by his physique rather than this spirit. He wrote back to his brother-in-law, 'What has poor Horatio done, who is so weak, that he, above all the rest, should be sent to rough it out at sea? But let him come, and the first time we go into action, a cannon-ball may knock off his head, and provide for him at once.' With this encouragement, at the age of just twelve Nelson quit school and embarked on his military career.

There is an affecting story – one that seems a degree more believable than tales of his childhood courage – of how, after wandering about looking lost, he arrived alone at his uncle's ship, the *Raisonnable*. His uncle was not yet there, and no one paid him the slightest attention until the following day.

In later years Nelson would often feel that insufficient attention was paid to him. Some heroes appear quite unselfconscious about their heroism, and to be self-effacing to the point of invisibility. Not so Nelson. He always sought recognition – and was not

Nelson's birthplace

much hindered by English reserve in the process. Though in some ways he had to grow up very fast, in other respects he never entirely grew up. He remained all his life in the thrall of an uncommon appetite for glory, coupled with a degree of emotional unguardedness that bordered upon naïvety. Indeed, in both public and private life he was driven by what were virtually obsessions. In his career this would be to his advantage; in his private life, especially after he had fallen in love with Emma Hamilton, it would come close to being his ruin.

'I WILL BE A HERO'

The *Raisonnable* had been commissioned to help deal with a Spanish threat to the Falkland Islands. As things turned out, Britain's differences with Spain were resolved without violence. Nelson's Uncle Maurice was reassigned to domestic guard duties on the Thames in the *Triumph*, a battleship of 74 guns, and according to the ship's muster book, the young Nelson went with him. In fact, he joined the merchant marine, and on a voyage to the West Indies was trained in seamanship. A story is told that he returned to his uncle, affected by a disillusion with the Royal Navy common among sailors, summed up in the slogan 'Aft the most honour; forward the better man', because the senior officers' quarters on a fighting ship were in the stern, while the men slung their hammocks forward. His uncle soon corrected him. But there was genuinely a great gulf between the officers and the men, and occasionally it could make itself felt – forcibly. Conditions in the navy were often very harsh, discipline severe, and the seamen sometimes forced into service. In Nelson's lifetime there would occur, in 1797, the Spithead and Nore mutinies, in which living conditions were a main bone of contention. Before then, in 1789, there had occurred the mutiny on the Bounty. While Nelson never sympathized with mutineers, one of his great gifts as a commander would prove to be his ability to inspire loyalty in his men.

In 1773, when he had not been back on the *Triumph* for long, he heard of an exploratory voyage in the Arctic. He was not yet fifteen, and the organizers had resolved that, because of the conditions they were likely to encounter, they would take no one under age. Nelson promptly persuaded Captain Lutwidge, the second-in-command, to take him anyway. Adventure beckoned, some opportunities presenting themselves naturally. At one point some officers, hunting a walrus, suddenly found themselves confronted by an enraged pack of the animals, who threatened to overturn their boat. Nelson was instrumental in saving them. A little later, he determined to bag a polar bear, and crept out on to the ice with a partner in crime in the middle of the night. As the fog cleared, the ship's watch was startled to see two figures confronting a vast bear. They were immediately signalled to return. Nelson, characteristically, remained, firing off the last of his ammunition, and then using his musket to try to club the beast to death. Lutwidge had one of the ship's guns fired, which frightened the animal off. The would-be hero explained, unabashed, 'Sir, I wished to kill the bear, that I might carry the skin home to my father.'

On his return Nelson resumed regular naval duties. In the autumn of 1773 he was assigned to the *Seahorse* and dispatched to the East Indies. He also started to move up the lowest rungs of the naval hierarchy; he became Able Seaman Nelson in the following spring, while still out east. His health, which was in any case never strong, suffered terribly, however.

By the end of the following year he was so completely in the grip of a fever that it was thought likely he would die. In those days of comparatively primitive medical care, the only remedy was to send him back on the long, gruelling journey home. So homewards he went in the *Dolphin*, managing finally to throw off the fever a few days before his homecoming.

His illness played some part in one of the formative moments of his life. Nelson would always be ambitious, and was often sustained by a powerful sense of destiny. These things coalesced to a point of utter despondency on the way home, when, as he explained: 'I felt impressed with a feeling that I should never rise in my profession. My mind was staggered with a view of the difficulties I had to surmount, and the little interest [i.e. influential friends] I possessed. I could discover no means of reaching the object of my ambition. After a long and gloomy reverie, in which I almost wished myself overboard, a sudden glow of patriotism was kindled within me, and presented my king and country as my patron. "Well, then," I exclaimed, "I will be a hero! and confiding in Providence, I will brave every danger!"'

Back home, his uncle did what he could for him, though without undue favouritism. He was assigned to the *Worcester* as acting lieutenant on convoy duties to Gibraltar and in the Mediterranean from September 1776 until the following April. On 8 April 1777 he faced his lieutenant's examination, even though he was technically too young – the minimum age for a lieutenant was twenty. Though his Uncle Maurice chaired the board, he was careful not to reveal his relation to the candidate until after the board had passed him. Nelson was then appointed to the *Lowestoffe* and sent to the West Indies. He continued to rise, being promoted to first lieutenant, and given his first command, the *Badger*, in December 1778, and then on 11 June 1779 he was promoted to post-captain and given command of the frigate *Hinchingbrooke*. The ship was still at sea, so while awaiting its return Nelson turned soldier for a while. This was the period of the American Revolution – a revolution which the French increasingly supported, and which also weakened Britain's position vis-à-vis other imperial powers in the region, notably Spain, which joined France in alliance with the American revolutionaries. A threatened invasion of the West Indies by a French army of 25,000 came to nothing, though Nelson was active in preparing defences in case it did. He then participated in an expedition to seize San Juan, the Spanish fort that commanded Lake Nicaragua, in the Spanish colony of the same name. He wasn't meant to have done more than ferry troops from the ships offshore to the mouth of the San Juan River, but, having nothing else to do while awaiting his command, decided he'd take them up the river as well. Conditions proved dire – not so much because of the enemy as of disease. Nelson did manage to participate in one action, however, an assault on a minor stronghold. Characteristically, even though he wasn't meant to be there, he was in the lead, leaping ashore and promptly losing his shoes in the squelching mud – he therefore stormed the battery barefoot.

Narrowly escaping being bitten by a venomous snake, he nevertheless went down with the fever that was decimating the expedition. They struggled on to the fort of San Juan. With the whole British forces on the point of succumbing to their maladies, the fort surrendered. But little good did it do the attackers, for soon there were not even enough healthy men left to bury the dead. Of the 1800 men who went upriver, no more than 380 returned. That Nelson survived at all was largely thanks to his being ordered back to Port Royal in Jamaica to assume his new command. He was so ill when he got there that there was nothing to do but send him home in the *Lion*.

After three months he felt sufficiently recovered to start pestering the Admiralty for sea duty. Early in 1781 he was appointed to command the *Albemarle*. Although his health had suffered a collapse, he was ordered to duty in the North Sea, and subsequently to Quebec. Among its duties the navy was to ensure that rebel Americans should not continue to trade with the same advantages they had enjoyed under British rule. On 14 July 1781, while patrolling the eastern seaboard of America, he captured the *Harmony*, a fishing vessel from Cape Cod, which happened to contain nearly all that her master, one Nathaniel Carver, possessed. Carver was pressed into service as a pilot in these unfamiliar waters. So well did he serve that Nelson restored him his vessel and cargo. A few months later the *Albemarle*'s supplies were running low, and the crew were afflicted with scurvy, when they happened once again upon the *Harmony*. Carver generously presented them with fresh supplies, and Nelson had a hard time inducing him to accept payment.

Even so, Nelson and this crew needed to return to Quebec to recuperate. Once there, the young captain promptly fell in love with sixteen-year-old Mary Simpson, and decided to quit the navy for her. A colleague found him on the beach when he ought to have been back on his ship, and managed to talk him out of it.

That he was prepared to contemplate leaving the navy at one moment did not in the least mean that his ambition was undimmed in the next. In 1782 he escorted a convoy to America, fetching up in New York at the same time as Admiral Lord Hood, who was bound for the West Indies. Never one to undervalue himself, Nelson secured a couple of interviews with the admiral, and demanded a better ship or better station, or both. He cut a somewhat unprepossessing figure – as Prince

Admiral Hood

William (later King William IV), who was serving under Hood noted, he was 'the merest boy of a captain'. But he got his wish, and was transferred south to the West Indies, where at least he might see action against the French.

Not for long, however, for hostilities with France ceased soon after, and the *Albemarle* was ordered back to Portsmouth to be paid off. As Nelson found, this was something of a euphemism, for though the men were laid off, he had an uphill struggle getting their back-pay for them. It was characteristic that he should make the attempt. Unlike most captains, he had made a point of personally selecting his crew, and of taking only volunteers.

After a jaunt to France (where he fell in love

again), he was soon back at sea. In 1784 he found himself commanding the *Boreas*, carrying his brother William as ship's chaplain, and taking Lady Hughes out to her husband, Admiral Sir Richard Hughes, in the Leeward Islands. Lady Hughes was impressed by the interest Nelson took in his crew's studies, and the encouragement he gave. In the case of a boy somewhat afraid to go aloft, he would say, 'Well, sir, I am going a race to the mast-head, and beg that I may meet you there.' Up Nelson would go, with the timid midshipman scrambling after. This instinct for cultivating other people's self-belief seldom deserted him.

However, his talent for cultivating his seniors' faith in him was a trifle more erratic. Though notorious for obeying only such orders as seemed good to him, he could be a stickler for discipline. Arriving in Antigua, he found a British frigate flying a commodore's pennant, and learning that the 'commodore' was actually a retired officer, temporarily authorized by Sir Richard Hughes to command, persisted in questioning the propriety of his flying a commodore's pennant. Sir Richard had also decided to wink at trade with the American rebels. Nelson was having none of this. It was in vain for Sir Richard to point out that he had had no particular orders about the trade; as Nelson pointed out the Acts were part of the statutes of the Admiralty. Additional pressure was brought to bear when aggrieved merchants brought a suit against him, suing him for the incredible sum of £40,000; indeed, the various lawsuits brought against him over this matter entangled him on and off for years. As if this was not enough, he started what was virtually a one-man crusade against corruption in the way in which the navy was supplied. Besides these problems, he was also involved in a couple of controversial disciplinary decisions. Nelson might have had great ambitions, but he had none of the talent for ingratiation that often goes with them.

In the midst of all this he met Mrs Nisbet, a doctor's widow with a three-year old son, Josiah, and married her. There is a touching and perhaps revealing record of Mr Herbert, president of the Nevis law court and uncle of Mrs Nisbet, going to receive Nelson, and finding him amusing little Josiah: 'Good God! if I did not find that great little man, of whom everybody is so afraid, playing in the next room, under the dining-table with Mrs Nisbet's child!' To his prospective wife, however, he sometimes showed the more austere side of his nature. 'Duty,' he wrote to her, 'is the great business of a sea officer: all private considerations must give way to it, however painful.' They were married on 11 March 1787. Later that same year he was ordered home and paid off. He would remain ashore in England for over five years, variously trying to sort out his lawsuits, and threatening to leave the country if the government did not support him in the legal wrangles in which he had been caught while on His Majesty's service.

'I WISH TO BE AN ADMIRAL'

Nelson was one of those military men who could not thrive in peacetime. This was not simply because superior officers tend to be killed off more quickly in time of war, thus speeding promotion, but because he was temperamentally unsuited to the tasks of peace. He lived largely on emotional energy; he was often sustained in battle by exhilaration, and, if the victory seemed less than complete, was prone to melancholy afterwards.

Fortunately for Nelson, war between Britain and France broke out again in 1793. In the wake of the French Revolution France had declared itself a republic, and promptly set about extending its territory and threatening British trade. Nelson was given command of the *Agamemnon*, a 64-gunner, and dispatched to the Mediterranean. At first he was elated – 'After the clouds comes sunshine', he declared. But when he found himself subject to commanders-in-chief of whom he did not approve, and obliged to execute a policy for which he felt little enthusiasm, his mood changed.

At first he was employed by Admiral Lord Hood in the blockade of Toulon, and was then peeved to be sent away from the prospect of action to raise troops in Naples. Here, in August, he met the British representative in Naples, Sir William Hamilton, and, fatefully, his wife Emma.

After briefly occupying Toulon (at which Nelson's opinion of Hood rose), the British withdrew to Corsica. The island was ruled by France, but the British plan was to make common cause with Corsican nationalists and expel the French. For this to happen, three fortresses would have to be seized. Nelson scented action, and partly by dint of deceiving his commander got orders to assault the fortress of Bastia. On 24 May 1794, after almost two months, it fell, much to Nelson's delight. He eagerly set about besieging the next fortress at Calvi, though somewhat irked that he had received no official commendation for his part in the fall of Bastia. Even so he was typically taking risks. On 12 July shrapnel and rock struck him in the face, his laconic report to Hood being 'I got a little hurt this morning.' He was never fully to recover the sight of his right eye. With the loss of Calvi, however, the French defeat in Corsica was complete.

The autumn found Nelson back at sea, and under a new commander-in-chief, Admiral William Hotham having replaced Hood. The following year Nelson discovered the shortcomings of his commander. In two engagements with the French fleet in March and July, with Nelson as usual in the lead, the British admiral broke off the attack before victory was complete. Hotham's attitude was 'We must be contented: we have done very well,' but this fell on deaf ears where Nelson was concerned. With some degree of self-knowledge he remarked: 'I wish to be an admiral, and in the command of the English fleet; I should very soon either do much, or be ruined: my disposition cannot bear tame and slow measures. Sure I am had I commanded on the 14th, that either the whole French fleet would have graced my triumph, or I should have been in a confounded scrape.'

In his frustration, Nelson resumed the financially risky business of stopping merchants trading with the French – risky because he was personally liable to be sued in the event of his stopping the wrong ships. Cheerfully unconcerned he went his own way, explaining to his wife: 'I am acting, not only without the orders of my commander-in-chief, but in some measure contrary to them. However, I have not only the support of His Majesty's Minister, both at Turin and Genoa, but a consciousness that I am doing right and proper for the service of our king and country.'

He was greatly heartened, therefore, when Hotham was replaced in January 1796 by Admiral Sir John Jervis, although as one colleague wryly observed, the identity of the commander-in-chief scarcely affected Nelson: 'You did just as you pleased in Lord Hood's time, the same in Admiral Hotham's, and now again with Sir John Jervis: it makes no difference to you who is commander-in-chief.'

Jervis's arrival brought promotion to the rank of commodore. But to Nelson's chagrin the war against the French, which was largely conducted by the Austrians, went badly, while the British continued to fall back, abandoning Corsica for Elba, and then quitting Elba too. Nelson fought a somewhat inconclusive engagement with a couple of Spanish frigates, as a result of which some British sailors, the crew of a French prize, were taken prisoner, among them one Lieutenant Thomas Hardy, who would accompany Nelson for much of the remainder of his life once the latter had negotiated his release.

Finally, in February 1797 came the kind of battle Nelson relished. Though heavily outnumbered by the Spanish fleet (Spain was allied to France), Jervis saw a way to win. The idea was to sail the fifteen British vessels under his command through the Spanish line, exploit his ships' superior manoeuvrability to keep the enemy divided in small groups, and then tackle them one at a time. He gave orders accordingly, and on 14 February, off Cape St Vincent, battle was joined.

Nelson's ship, the *Captain*, was in the rear of the British column. From his position he could see that the Spanish line was starting to re-form after the initial assault more quickly than had been anticipated. With reckless courage, and flagrant disregard for his orders, he pulled the *Captain* out of the line and made all speed to intervene to keep the Spanish line broken. This brought him up against seven Spanish vessels, most of them more heavily armed than his own. The battle around the *Captain* was so fierce that her sails and wheel were shot away. Though his ship was almost impossible to steer, Nelson managed to come alongside the *San Nicolas*, which he and his men boarded. Then when the *San Josef*, a larger ship, drew alongside the *San Nicolas* to relieve her, Nelson boarded that too, crossing from one Spanish ship to the other, a technique which his admiring crew dubbed

'Nelson's patent bridge for boarding first rates'. They had paid a heavy price, however, a quarter of all the British casualties in the battle were sustained by the crew of the *Captain*.

Nelson himself was only bruised – but he had yet to face the commander whose orders he had disobeyed. Jervis's fleet captain, Robert Calder, considered that Nelson ought to be disciplined. Jervis chose instead to welcome his disobedient hero with thanks and praise, but significantly failed to extend these in his official account of the battle. Even so, a grateful country showered honours on its victorious sailors. Jervis became Earl St Vincent, and Nelson became a Knight of the Bath. Ironically, in view of his earlier wish to become an admiral, on 3 February, a few days before the battle, he had

Battle of Cape St Vincent, 1797

been promoted to the rank of rear-admiral, though news of this did not reach him until after the action.

'VICTORY IS NOT A NAME STRONG ENOUGH FOR SUCH A SCENE'

In April 1797 Nelson was given command of the Mediterranean inshore squadron. He was still under Jervis (now St Vincent), but was allowed a pretty free hand. Indeed, when Vice-Admiral Sir John Orde complained at the freedom Nelson was allowed, he was sent straight home.

However, the first action Nelson was

Action off Cadiz, July 1797

involved in as an admiral was the kind he chafed at. A Spanish fleet had taken refuge in Cadiz, and Nelson was ordered to blockade the town and try to lure them into battle. The motive for this was in part to keep discipline within the British navy itself. A spirit of discontent was abroad among the men (some were executed for mutiny), and action was deemed the best way to quell it. That said, Nelson himself had a salutary effect upon morale. His new ship, the *Theseus*, had just come from England under Captain Miller, and was thought to be rife with troublemakers. After less than a month of Nelson's command an anonymous paper was found on the quarterdeck, which read: 'Success attend Admiral Nelson! God bless Captain Miller! We thank them for the officers they have placed over us. We are happy and comfortable and will shed every drop of blood in our veins to support them, and the name of *Theseus* shall be immortalized as high as the *Captain*'s SHIPS COMPANY.'

Bored by the stand-off at Cadiz, Nelson greeted the chance to attempt a conclusive bombardment on 3 July. In the course of the assault Nelson was attacked in his admiral's barge by a similar, though more heavily manned, Spanish vessel, and had to engage in a hand-to-hand fight in which his coxswain, John Sykes, twice saved his life. He later remarked, 'My personal courage was more conspicuous than at any other period of my life,' and concluded that Sykes had shown such spirit that nature must have intended him to be a gentleman. By the end of the fight eighteen of a Spanish crew of thirty lay dead.

All to no avail. Not only did Cadiz not fall,

but would-be mutineers in ships other than Nelson's were not much deterred. Disciplinary executions continued.

Nelson was then ordered, that same July, to Tenerife, in the Canary Islands, to try to capture a Spanish treasure ship. The mission proved disastrous. He decided to try to surprise the batteries protecting the port of Santa Cruz, trusting to the element of surprise to even the odds. When this was lost, he went ahead anyway, leading the attack personally. He had scarcely stepped ashore when grapeshot caught his right arm round the elbow. As he fell, he deftly caught in his left hand the sword he had been holding in his right. His stepson, Josiah Nisbet, hauled him into a boat, applied a tourniquet, and set about getting him to safety. The Spanish guns had by now opened up in earnest, and, in the

Nelson, 1797

midst of his agony, Nelson noticed one of his ships was sinking. He ordered the boat carrying him to pick up survivors. Then, just as they were nearing the *Seahorse*, the closest ship on which he could receive the medical attention he urgently needed, he remembered that the captain's newly-wed wife was on board. He decided it would not do to alarm her by being seen in his present state, ignoring warnings that delay might prove fatal: 'Then I will die,' he said, 'I would rather suffer death than alarm Mrs Freemantle.' Even when they finally arrived at the *Theseus*, though he was weak with loss of blood and knew he faced amputation with nothing more than a stiff drink for anaesthetic, he insisted on climbing aboard himself. The arm off, and the disastrous battle done, Nelson succumbed to despondency and was sent home to recuperate.

He arrived in England in September, and went to visit his ailing father in Bath. He was far from well himself. He was in constant pain and for several months could sleep only with the help of doses of laudanum.

Finally, the prospect of a new ship and a return to action in the Mediterranean helped to heal his arm. By the following May he was back under St Vincent's command. He was required first of all to try to ascertain the objectives of the French fleet in Toulon, and then, when Napoleon Bonaparte, who had been given command of an invasion of Egypt by the Revolutionary government, managed to get the fleet out of port under cover of a sudden storm, he was to find and destroy it. Unfortunately, that same storm dismasted Nelson's flagship, the *Vanguard*, and separated him from his frigates, which were vital for the kind of reconnaissance work he now had to do. There followed a frustrating few weeks of sailing around the Mediterranean, trying to second-guess French intentions with little information to go on. At the end of June Nelson arrived in Alexandria, but couldn't find the French there. He continued his search. Then at last, at the end of July, he got wind of Bonaparte – he was indeed making for Egypt. He made full sail for Alexandria again, and finally sighted the enemy on 1 August, joining battle with them on that day.

The French position seemed impregnable. Vice-Admiral François Brueys d'Aigaïllers had anchored his fleet in Aboukir Bay at the mouth of the Nile. His ships were strung out in line of battle, anchored amidst shoals and shallows that made it very unlikely that anyone without the most accurate charts

Battle of the Nile, 1798

would be able to get around them, while to the front of them was the small Bequier Island, with a battery on it. Nelson, it is true, did not have charts showing the shoals. But that did not discourage him. As one of his captains recalled: 'It instantly struck his eager, penetrating mind, that where there was room for an Enemy's ship to swing, there was room for one of ours to anchor.' He was right. He was able to swing in, around the shoals – though his friend Captain Thomas Troubridge's vessel, the *Culloden*, was stranded – make for the most westerly end of the French line, and then work his way along it, concentrating the full firepower of his ships on just a few of the enemy at a time, attacking them from the landward side. The French were wholly unprepared for such a move. The battle began at about 6.30 p.m. Some two hours later Nelson received a head wound, which caused a flap of skin to fall over his good eye, temporarily blinding him. About an hour-and-a-half later Bruey's flagship, *L'Orient*, exploded, killing him and almost all aboard, and taking Napoleon's treasure and loot to the bottom of the bay. According to Edward Berry, Nelson's flag captain, after this terrific explosion there was 'an awful pause and death-like silence for about three minutes' – broken by the sound of *L'Orient*'s masts and yards dropping into the sea from the immense height to which they had been blown. Then the battle resumed. It was to rage for four hours yet, but already, with his head stitched up and in intense pain, Nelson had written a dispatch to St Vincent announcing his success: 'Victory is not a name strong enough for such a scene.' Napoleon's army was now isolated in Egypt.

Sword given to Nelson in honour of the Battle of the Nile

At last he had won a great victory on his own account. A grateful nation was not slow to show its appreciation. The East India Company, appreciating that Nelson had hindered Napoleon's threatening eastward advance on British India, gave him £10,000. His captains were knighted, and he was made Baron Nelson of the Nile. The King of Naples, Ferdinand, delighted and relieved, made him Duke of Bronte. He also received gifts from the Sultan of Turkey and the Tsar of Russia, and was henceforth a national hero.

NAPLES

Nelson limped back to Naples in what was left of the *Vanguard*, with his head in agony, and for a time succumbing to a fever which it was feared would kill him. In Naples he was accorded an elaborately ceremonious and, so far as the court was concerned, highly emotional hero's welcome. Though Emma Hamilton had only met him once, briefly, five years before, she felt intensely concerned for his success. When the barge carrying her to greet the returning fleet came alongside the

Naples

Vanguard, as she saw Nelson she 'sprang up the ship's side, exclaiming "O God! is it possible!" and fell into his arms – more, he says, like one dead than alive.'

Such lack of reserve may seem surprising in an English lady, but Emma Hamilton had not always been a lady. Born plain Emma Lyon, she was the daughter of a Cheshire blacksmith, and had been mistress to a succession of young gentlemen and rakes. In the course of her career she had picked up the ways of polite society, and in 1786 finally passed from Charles Greville to his uncle, Sir William Hamilton, who, somewhat to the world's surprise, married her five years later. History has enshrined her as a beautiful *femme fatale*. But she could often be course, and some accounts, less flattering than the miniature Nelson used to carry, speak of a very large, if well-proportioned, woman, except for her feet, which were apparently enormous.

Why should Nelson, who until this moment had been a loyal and affectionate husband, have proved susceptible to Emma? He himself would later assert that Lady Hamilton had done her country a great service in securing the stores his fleet had needed to defeat Brueys by using her influence with the Queen of Naples. It might be argued that she gave him a kind of unabashed hero-worship which his wife was not in a position to give, and which met a particular need of Nelson's. But perhaps the truth of the matter is that, like Nelson himself, her emotions readily came to the surface. Nelson's whole temperament was dependent to an unusual extent upon emotional stimulation to keep him from ill

Lady Hamilton

health and the kind of despondency to which he occasionally succumbed after battle or when starved of its prospect. Marriage, by its domestic nature was ill equipped to meet this need, but *une grande affaire* was a plausible substitute.

The very frustration of life in Naples may have driven him to make his own kind of (emotional) action. Like other English officers, his views of the Neapolitans, and especially of their courage, were little short of racist. He deemed the people as a whole degenerate and cowardly. There was little to be done at sea while French forces under General Championnet advanced through the Italian mainland, most of which they had by now conquered. The Neapolitan army was large, but its quality and its leadership were poor; as Nelson observed when that army fled before the French, 'The officers did not lose much honour, for God knows they had not much honour to lose, but they lost all they had.' The army routed, Nelson carried the royal family to safety in Sicily just before Christmas Day. Early in 1799 Naples as a whole fell under French control, and was reconstituted as the Parthenopian Republic.

While Nelson periodically put to sea in search of a second French fleet, Cardinal Fabrizio Ruffo, royal vicar of Naples, succeeded in raising a revolt against the French on the mainland. By the middle of 1799 Ruffo's success was such that he was prepared to negotiate the withdrawal of the French and their Neapolitan supporters from their strongholds. A truce was followed by an agreement signed by, among others, Captain Edward Foote of the Royal Navy, which would have secured this. Then Nelson arrived in the bay of Naples. He was little inclined to honour an agreement made by an untrustworthy and cowardly Papist with a bunch of untrustworthy and rebellious Papists and the archenemy, the French. Any doubts he may have had were banished by a message from Queen Maria Carolina, relayed by Lady Hamilton, urging him 'to treat Naples as if it were a rebellious Irish town'. He proceeded to act with exactly that disregard for principle and humanity that has too often characterized English conduct in Ireland. He decided to set aside the agreement. Garrisons which had surrendered, having negotiated their safe conduct and honourable treatment, found themselves arrested and dispatched to suffer vengeance at the hands of their royalist enemies. Admiral Prince Caracciolo, sometime commander of the Neapolitan Navy, having returned to occupied Naples with his king's blessing to secure his estates, had served the Parthenopian Republic, albeit under duress. He attempted to slip away in disguise. He was arrested at nine in the morning of 24 June; at Nelson's instigation a court martial of Neapolitan officers was convened by a man who happened to be Caracciolo's enemy; sentence was passed; by five that afternoon Caracciolo was swinging from the yardarm of the *Minerva*. Nelson was deaf to his pleas for justice, for delay of execution, and even for an alternative mode of execution. His corpse was weighted and cast into the bay.

Meanwhile St Vincent had been replaced as C-in-C by Admiral Lord Keith. Keith, aware of the possibility of a French attack on Minorca, in July ordered Nelson to defend it. Nelson flatly refused. How far it was sound judgement or mere good luck is hard to determine, but fortunately for Nelson the French did not attack Minorca. Had they done so, his disobedience would have ensured the end of his career.

Finally, the following spring Sir William was replaced as British Minister in Naples. To the dismay of his friends, Nelson was now blatantly infatuated with Emma. He requested home leave in order to recover his health, and in April 1800 set off home with the Hamiltons across Europe, the focus of attention wherever he went. Keith was glad to see him go. As he observed, 'Lady Hamilton [had] had command of the fleet long enough.'

'I REALLY DO NOT SEE THE SIGNAL'

Back in England Nelson attracted a mixture of notoriety and hero-worship. His liaison with Lady Hamilton, which Sir William astonishingly seemed to countenance, inevitably brought matters to a head with his wife. Though Nelson continued to observe certain formalities to her, soon after his return they separated, Nelson apparently blind to the humiliation he inflicted upon her. The Admiralty looked askance at their irregular hero. Had there not been a war to fight his career might have petered out. As it was they chose to employ him, but with the significant slight of making him second-in-command of a force that was to pre-empt the anticipated hostility of a League of Northern States (Russia, Denmark, Prussia, Sweden), who were disgruntled at British highhandedness at sea – a disgruntlement Napoleon hoped to exploit. In any case, the League represented a threat to British trade. The Baltic expedition was to go to Denmark in the first instance, stand by while a diplomatic solution was attempted, and if that failed, attack.

At the end of January 1801, even as Nelson was ordered to serve under Admiral Sir Hyde Parker, Lady Hamilton was giving birth to twins. Only one of them survived and – a broad hint as to her paternity – was christened Horatia. This was somewhat surprising, given the lengths to which Nelson went to deny the nature of his relationship – including swearing a solemn oath in church that he and Emma were not lovers, and distributing bibles to every member of the crew of his flagship, all 834 of them! Their affair was in any case common knowledge, largely because Nelson could not help but devote his whole attention to Emma when in her company. Even so, their transparent pretences continued.

Nelson doted on his daughter, proudly declaring, 'A finer child never was produced by any two persons.' Almost the last thing he did before the Baltic expedition got under way was to dash back to London to see the infant. Then, hurrying back to his flagship, the *Elephant*, he wrote to reassure Emma that

Nelson by Hoppner

she was his wife 'in my eyes and in the face of heaven'. The inconvenient circumstance that both of them were married to other people, he simply set aside. He sailed first to Yarmouth to collect troops, and on 12 March they set sail.

Nelson was irked not to be kept fully informed of Parker's orders and the nature of their expedition. At the end of the month it was clear that his special talents would be called upon: they would have to fight the Danes. The enemy fleet was in a strong position: overlooked by shore batteries, with the added zest that comes from defending one's homeland, and with lines of supply as short as possible. They were strung out in line of battle in front of Copenhagen, while before them was a treacherous shallow called Middle Ground which seemed further to reduce the scope for action by the British, who had no charts of the shoals.

Nelson, however, was undeterred. He spent nights out in a longboat personally taking the soundings of the channel along which he would lead his force, and from the direction the Danes least expected. On the afternoon of 1 April 1801 he sailed around the Middle Ground on the far side, arriving at the southerly end of the Danish line by dusk. Obligingly, the wind then turned. The plan was, as at the Nile, to sail up the enemy line, directing the concentration of fire on successive parts of it.

However, the Battle of Copenhagen did not go quite so smoothly. In the early stages of the battle three of Nelson's twelve ships of the line ran ground as they tried to sail between the Danish fleet and Middle Ground. The Danes fought spiritedly, and British return of fire was not as effective as it might have been because the need to avoid the shallows kept them from their optimum firing positions. A squadron of frigates under Captain Edward Riou had the unequal task of keeping some of the land batteries occupied, and suffered heavy punishment, Riou himself being killed. To Admiral Parker, stationed at some little distance, and unable to approach closer because of the winds, it seemed that he must try to salvage what he could of his force. He signalled withdrawal, though, realizing that Nelson might well disobey him, he generously remarked, 'I will make a signal to recall for Nelson's sake. If he is in a condition to continue the action successfully he will disregard it: if he is not it will be an excuse for his retreat and no blame can be imputed to him.'

Nelson considered himself to be in the most terrible battle he had ever known, but he had no intention of breaking off. As usual, in the thick of action he was elated. When Parker made the signal, the frigates obeyed, while Nelson's second-in-command, Admiral Thomas Graves, repeated his C-in-C's signal, but without ceasing also to fly signal no. 16, 'Close Action'. When Nelson received Parker's signal, he was in no mood to obey. He told his flag captain, Thomas Foley, 'Leave off action? Now damn me if I do! . . . You know, Foley, I have only one eye. I have a right to be blind sometimes.' Then, clapping the telescope to his bad eye, he announced, 'I really do not see the signal.'

The outcome of the battle did not quite match Nelson's elation. The fortune of the day did swing his way, ironically at the very moment that Parker ordered a general disengagement. But casualties were heavy: a thousand British dead, and two to six times that number among the Danes. Nonetheless, ceasefire was succeeded in due course by a treaty.

The work of the Baltic expedition was not quite done, however, for the Swedes and Russians remained. After an inconclusive action against a Swedish force, on 5 May Sir Hyde Parker was replaced as commander-in-chief by Nelson. Nelson sought to ensure that the Swedish and Russian fleets could not combine by leaving the greater part of his force to watch the Swedes, while he went north to find the Russians. However, his mission was called off when the murder of Tsar Paul I and his succession by Alexander I brought a complete change of Russian policy. The new Tsar sent messages of goodwill to Nelson. No longer needed at sea, suffering from the despondency that sometimes followed action, and in poor health, Nelson headed for home.

'ENGLAND EXPECTS . . .'

He was duly honoured for his victory by being made Viscount Nelson of the Nile and Burnham Thorpe. After a few weeks the Admiralty, eager to distract him from Emma, charged him with routine defensive work. Then there followed a relatively long period at home. He purchased a farm at Merton (nowadays part of south London), and in the autumn of 1801 took up residence there with Sir William and Lady Hamilton. His father lived there too for the few months before his

Victory

death in April 1802. A month earlier, war between Britain and France had ended with the Treaty of Amiens. Domestic peace was somewhat ruffled by financial problems (which he would never resolve), but their sting was softened by his continuing popularity in the county at large. Then, on 6 April 1803, Sir William, either a remarkably complacent or a remarkably forgiving man, died with his wife at his side, and Nelson holding his hand.

This interlude of peace ended with the renewal of hostilities between Britain and France the following month; later, Spain joined France as an ally. Nelson was soon back in the Mediterranean, but now as C-in-C, with his flag in the *Victory*, and with orders, as he had had years before, to bottle up a French fleet in Toulon. This time the

French were commanded by Admiral Count Louis de Latouche-Tréville, who had scored some success two years before by repulsing an attack on Boulogne under Nelson's ultimate command, though he had not led the expedition personally. Nelson forbore to launch an all-out assault upon a fleet so strongly placed, and contented himself with driving it back to port when it ventured forth. There it stayed until Latouche-Tréville's death in August 1804.

The cat-and-mouse game continued under his successor, Admiral Pierre de Villeneuve. Nelson, unable to fight the enemy, was fighting on other fronts: against his own poor health, and against an old rival, Vice-Admiral Orde, to whom the Admiralty had given a new command to the west of Gibraltar, and for whom, ever since Orde's complaints about him in 1797, Nelson had little time. Villeneuve made a serious effort to dodge past Nelson on New Year's Day 1805, only to be beaten back by the weather. A second attempt at the end of March succeeded.

Napoleon, who the previous year had crowned himself emperor, was planning an invasion of Britain, for which he needed to concentrate his own naval forces, while decoying and dispersing the British. Villeneuve followed a plan designed to accomplish this. He would make for the West Indies, luring Nelson into following him, join with other French forces, and briefly seize the opportunity to obstruct British shipping in the region before recrossing the Atlantic to ferry Napoleon's army over the English Channel with the assistance of the fleet of his Spanish allies.

It got off to a good start. Villeneuve broke out of port and headed west; Nelson, falling prey to poor intelligence, headed east. When he realized his error he did exactly what Villeneuve wanted: he followed west. However, he did so at a speed that bewildered the French. Nelson only turned westwards five weeks after Villeneuve had broken the blockade – a few days before the French fleet's arrival in Martinique. Villeneuve had arrived, with sickness rife in his fleet, after a journey of nearly six weeks; Nelson made the same journey in just under three. Having failed to join forces with the other French fleets as planned, Villeneuve recrossed the ocean and united with a Spanish squadron on 2 August, only to find that Nelson had beaten him on the return leg, and was already in Gibraltar. Britain was suitably impressed, and Nelson's star shone more brightly than ever, as he discovered during nearly a month of shore leave.

Events on the Continent combined to make Napoleon shelve his invasion plans, as he pulled back much of his army to meet an Austro–Russian threat, which he finally defeated at the Battle of Austerlitz – perhaps the masterpiece of his career. However, he had left a large enough force in Boulogne to delude his enemies into supposing that the invasion would still take place.

On 15 September, a fortnight after the bulk of Napoleon's invasion force had quit Boulogne, Nelson left England for the last time. Thirteen days later he rejoined the fleet. As he had done before the Battle of the Nile, he discussed his plans fully with his captains, his 'Band of Brothers' as he referred to them, as

Shakespeare's Henry V speaks of his army. They warmed to such treatment.

They had the enemy blockaded in Cadiz. Villeneuve was under pressure from Napoleon to venture forth.

Meanwhile Nelson was trying to coax the Franco–Spanish fleet into combat by pretending his force was diminished or scattered. Finally, on 19 October, Villeneuve took the bait. One part of his force sailed that day, the remainder on the morrow.

The seamanship of the Franco–Spanish fleet could not match that of the British. Villeneuve struggled in vain to get his force into formation. Shortly after dawn on 21 October Nelson ordered his force to divide into two columns, following the plan he had

Admiral Collingwood

previously agreed with his captains. One column under Vice-Admiral Cuthbert Collingwood would engage the enemy's rear, while the other under Nelson would divide the enemy line in two, engage the middle, and keep the van occupied. The British ships moved as planned. Those of Villeneuve, already in difficulties, were further disconcerted when at 8 a.m. he ordered them back to Cadiz.

Nelson meanwhile occupied himself with alterations to his will (in an attempt to get the state to provide for Lady Hamilton should he be killed), offering a final prayer, having something to eat, and making a tour of inspection. Shortly before action was joined he ordered that 'England Confides That Every Man Will Do His Duty' be signalled to the fleet. It was pointed out to him that since

Battle of Trafalgar, 1805

there was no single flag for 'Confides' would he accept 'Expects' instead? He would. The amended signal was made.

Collingwood's column went into action a few minutes before Nelson's, just before noon. At 12.08 Collingwood broke through the enemy line. The rest of his column, sailing in tight formation, soon followed.

At 12.10 the Franco–Spanish fleet opened fire upon the *Victory*, Nelson's flagship, at the head of his column. Because Nelson was sailing straight at the enemy, he couldn't bring his guns to bear upon them without turning. For fourteen minutes he was under fire, without being able to return it. In those fourteen minutes 50 of his crew were killed, and the wheelhouse was destroyed. At 12.30 the *Victory* rammed Villeneuve's flagship,

Redoubtable. The enemy was already in disarray, and the signals by which Villeneuve sought to regroup and concentrate his forces were so inexact as to add to his fleet's disorder.

At 1.15 the chaplain on the *Victory*, Dr Alexander Scott, emerged from the cockpit where the wounded were being tended, and went on deck. As Nelson's flag captain, Hardy, turned to him he beheld a sight he'd dreaded. Admiral Nelson had fallen to his knees. He had been hit by a sniper's ball: fired from the rigging of the *Redoubtable*. It had struck him about his left epaulette, and continued inwards. In a dress uniform, albeit a battered one, and with all his insignia, Nelson had made a conspicuous target. 'They have done for me, Hardy,' he said, 'My backbone is shot through.' It was a sadly accurate

Nelson mortally wounded

diagnosis. Covering him with handkerchiefs, lest the sight of him dishearten the men, Hardy had him carried below.

There, as the battle raged, Nelson spent the next three hours dying. It was soon apparent that there was little to be done for him. Hardy visited him twice, and the second time he was able to congratulate Nelson upon 'a brilliant victory'. Hardy had already advised Collingwood of their stricken commander's condition, but Nelson was loath to relinquish command, insisting on the need to anchor. Then a thought struck him: 'Don't throw me overboard, Hardy.' It was a moment before Hardy could master his feelings sufficiently to reassure his friend. Nelson's thoughts then resumed a familiar course: 'Take care of my dear Lady Hamilton, Hardy; take care of poor Lady Hamilton – Kiss me, Hardy.' Hardy kissed him on the cheek. 'Now I am satisfied. Thank God, I have done my duty.'

A moment later Hardy kissed him on the forehead. 'Who is that?' Nelson asked. He was told. 'God bless you, Hardy.' In his last minutes he confided to Dr Scott, 'Doctor, I have not been a great sinner,' and then urged once more that it be remembered that he left Lady Hamilton and Horatia as 'a legacy to my country'. His final words were 'Thank God I have done my duty.' At half-past four he died.

By then the battle was virtually over, though the last shot was not fired until an hour later. The British had captured Villeneuve and eighteen enemy vessels (Nelson had predicted twenty). Only a handful of those that escaped were ever fit for action again. Admiral Pierre Dumanoir managed to get four ships away,

Nelson's funeral procession

only to see them captured by a British squadron on 4 November. Napoleon's hopes of an invasion of Britain were forever dashed.

Nelson's body was brought home for a hero's funeral and a burial in St Paul's – as he himself would have liked, having calculated that the dry ground of the cathedral would rot his carcass less swiftly than the damps of Westminster Abbey. Honours and gifts were showered upon his surviving relations. His hereditary titles descended to his brother William, who was made an earl for good measure, and did what he could to help Lady Hamilton. But officialdom ignored Nelson's dying requests, and, having fled her debts, Emma died in penury and obscurity in Calais in 1815.

More than his titles, however, more than the

official funeral, Nelson was commemorated in the hearts of the thousands who mourned him, and the millions since who have read his story, and admired and felt for him. No one could pretend he had been a perfect man; but no one doubted he had been their hero.